Kids Ask

WHY?

WHY do cats have whiskers?

WHY do some people have freckles?

WHY don't boats sink?

sequoia™
children's publishing

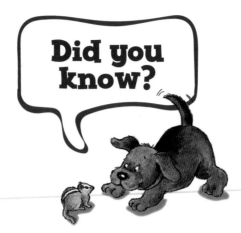

Illustrated by Tammie Lyon

Photography © Shutterstock 2021 LilKar; Steve Heap; Nikolai Danilenko;
Eric Isselee; Yellow Cat; Bahadir Yeniceri; Soyka; Fevziie; 2happy; irin-k;
JLStock; Egoreichenkov Evgenii; noraismail; Odua Images;
VanWagner; Ermolaev Alexander
Photography © iStock ValentynVolkov

Published by Sequoia Children's Publishing,
a division of Phoenix International Publications, Inc.

8501 West Higgins Road   59 Gloucester Place   Heimhuder Straße 81
Chicago, Illinois 60631   London W1U 8JJ   20148 Hamburg

© 2021 Sequoia Publishing & Media, LLC

Customer Service: cs@sequoiakidsbooks.com

www.sequoiakidsbooks.com

ISBN 978-1-64269-350-8

Kids ask WHY?

Table of Contents

WHY do some trees change color in autumn?

Trees use sunlight to make food. This makes the leaves green. In the fall, trees stop making food. The leaves lose their green color. They will have new green leaves in the spring!

WHY do trees have bark?

Bark is like skin for a tree. It protects the tree from wind, heat, and cold. Each tree has its own special pattern in its bark, like a fingerprint.

WHY do cats have whiskers?

Cats use their whiskers to feel if something is near their face. This helps keep them safe. Cats can tell with their whiskers if they will fit through a small hole.

WHY do puppies sniff everything?

Dogs use their sense of smell to learn all about the world. To puppies, the world is new and exciting! They need to smell everything and everyone they meet.

Did you know?

Dogs have an amazing sense of smell. Some kinds of dogs can use their noses to help find people who are lost. Others can smell if someone is sick!

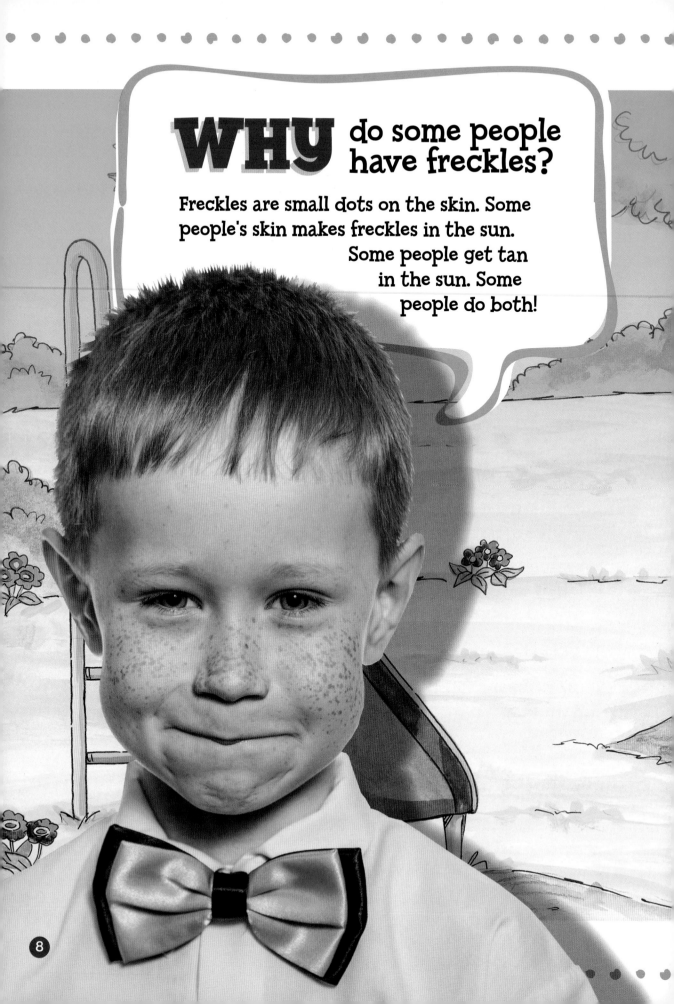

WHY do some people have freckles?

Freckles are small dots on the skin. Some people's skin makes freckles in the sun. Some people get tan in the sun. Some people do both!

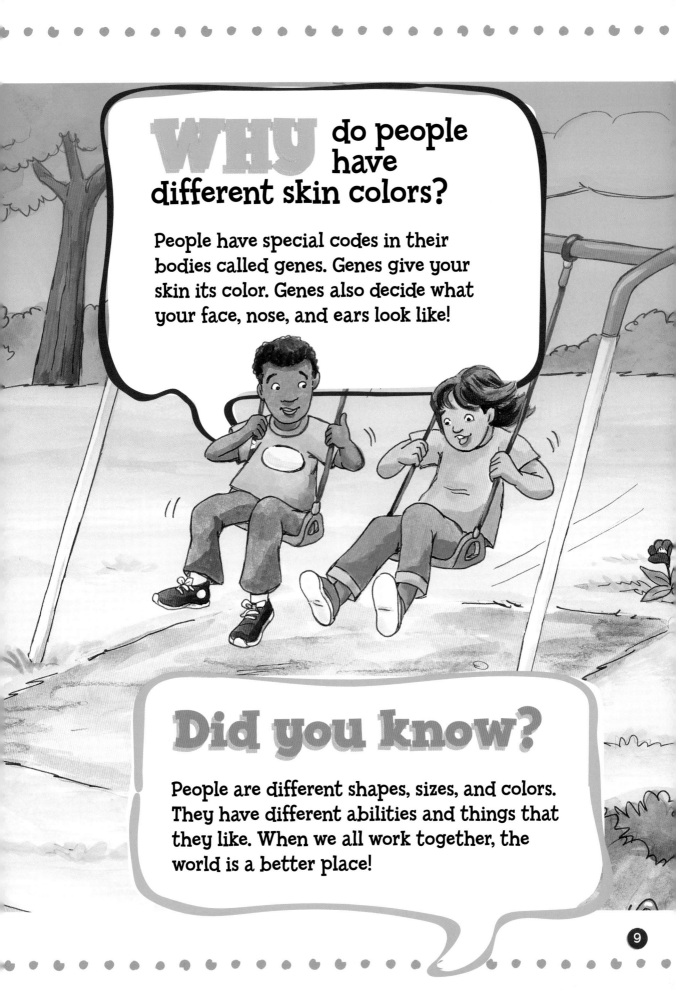

WHY do people have different skin colors?

People have special codes in their bodies called genes. Genes give your skin its color. Genes also decide what your face, nose, and ears look like!

Did you know?

People are different shapes, sizes, and colors. They have different abilities and things that they like. When we all work together, the world is a better place!

WHY do bees sting?

Bees sting when they are afraid. It is their way of telling people and animals to stay away next time. This is how bees protect themelves.

Did you know?

The honey we eat is made by bees. Honeybees make honey in the summer and store it for food in the winter. They make the honey from the nectar in flowers.

WHY are flowers colorful?

Birds and bees like bright colors. When birds and bees go from flower to flower, they move pollen from one flower to another. This is how new flowers grow!

WHY don't spiders get caught in their own webs?

Some of the threads in a web are sticky, and some are not. When an insect touches the web, it gets stuck on the sticky part. The spider runs down the other threads to get it.

WHY do ants live in big groups?

Ants work together. Some ants get food for the whole group. Some build the group's home. Some take care of all the babies. Ants cannot live outside of their group.

Did you know?

Ants "talk" to each other by using smells. Ants leave a trail of smells to lead other ants to food. That's why you see ants marching all in a row.

WHY does the moon change shape?

The moon doesn't really change shape. We just see different parts of it at different times. When the sun is facing the moon, we see the full moon.

WHY
do owls come out at night?

Different animals live in different ways. Owls sleep in the daytime and hunt mice and other small animals at night. Owls can see in the dark and hear very well.

Did you know?

The smallest type of owl is the elf owl. It is about as big as your hand and weighs less than a hamburger.

WHY don't boats sink?

Boats are lighter than water. This is because boats are full of air. The air keeps the boat from sinking. If the boat gets a leak and fills up with water, it will sink.

Did you know?

Submarines are a kind of boat that can go underwater. Parts of the submarine fill with water to make it heavy. When it needs to come back up, sailors let the water out.

WHY do I sometimes get a shock when I pet my dog?

Electricity is a type of energy. When the air is dry, static electricity can build up on things. When you touch a person or thing, it can make a spark.

WHY does a lightbulb light up?

All types of lightbulbs use electricity. One kind has a thin wire in it. The wire gets hot and glows. Other kinds use gases or metals. These make light but do not get hot.

WHY do I need to sleep at night?

All people and animals have to sleep. Sleeping helps our bodies and brains get ready for the next day. We need sleep in order to grow, think, and play.